The Sous Vide Method made simple

The Sous Vide Cookbook for Absolute Beginners with Tasty, Healthy and Easy to Follow Recipes

Jonathan Mckennie

Table of Content

Dessert Recipes 106

Introduction

From fast-foods to the British Royal Navy! All of them utilize this technique to get the perfect meal every single time.

Just in case you are wondering, there is no secret "magical" spell behind all of these. It's a simple matter of consistent heating.

Ever since the olden days, human beings have tried to control and tame the powers of heat for braising, sealing, roasting, keeping them warm and, of course, cooking!

Thanks to the desire of Man to control the power of fire, culinary evolutions have given birth to the stove, ovens and even the very simple yet useful temperature dials!

And it is, throughout these steps of innovation, that the honorable method of Sous Vide came into existence.

The origin of Sous Vide lies in the mid 1970's when a famous chef known as Georges Praulus developed the technique simply as a means of trying to minimize costly shrinkage, and create an optimal environment for cooking the extremely luxurious foie gras.

Later on, this technique was enhanced by Chef Bruno Goussault who adopted this technique and started to cater to the first-class travelers of Air France by creating meals that simply left them spellbound.

Breakfast

Recipes

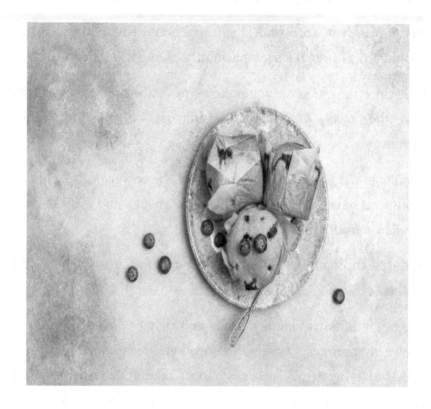

Toast with Avocado and Eggs

Preparation time: 5 minutes Cooking time: 10 minutes Servings: 1

Ingredients:

- 2 slices of bread (preferably multigrain or brown bread
- 1/2 teaspoon cinnamon powder
- 1 avocado
- 1 egg
- 1 teaspoon butter
- Cheese
- Salt to taste

Directions:

1. Toast the bread slices in the toaster.

2. Take an avocado and peel it. Remove the pit.

3. Mash the avocado with a masher or with hands and spread it evenly on the bread slices.

4. Set the sous vide machine to 135 degrees Fahrenheit.

5. Take a ziplock bag, add beat the egg, add little salt and pepper. Remove air and seal.

6. Submerge this bag in water bath and heat for 5 minutes.

7. Take a bread toast with avocado spread and place a cheese slice on it.

8.   Add the poached egg on the avocado spread toast.

9.   Sprinkle salt and cinnamon powder on it and serve hot.

Nutrition: calories 322lcal.

Blueberry Coconut Gluten Free Waffles

Preparation time: 5 minutes Cooking time: 10 minutes Servings: 4

Ingredients:

- 1 cup coconut flour

- 2 tablespoon almond flour

- 1/2 teaspoon cinnamon powder

- 1/2 teaspoon cardamom powder

- 1/2 cup coconut milk

- Fresh blueberries

- Fresh mint leaves

- Sour cream

- 1 tablespoon honey

- Salt to taste

Directions:

1.   Take a large mixing bowl, add the coconut flour, almond flour, cinnamon powder, cardamom powder and mix thoroughly.

2.   To this mixture add salt, honey and coconut milk to make a smooth batter.

3.   Crush few (5-6 blueberries using hand and add to the above mixture.

4.   Mix the batter properly to avoid any lumps.

5.   Grease the waffle iron using butter or

cooking spray.

6.   Pour a spoonful of the above batter into the waffle maker and allow it to turn golden brown.

7.   Set the sous vide machine to 145 degrees Fahrenheit.

8.   Take a ziplock bag, add the fresh blueberries and sprinkle powdered sugar. Remove air and seal.

9.   Submerge this bag in water bath and heat for 5 minutes.

10.   Layer the hot waffle with sour cream, sugared blueberries and fresh mint and serve it hot.

Nutrition: calories 128kcal per waffle.

Blueberry Dates Pancakes

Preparation time: 5 minutes Cooking time: 20 minutes Servings: 6

Ingredients:

- 1 cup almond flour

- 1 cup coconut flour

- 1 cup almond milk

- 10 dates

- 1/2 teaspoon cinnamon powder

- 2 tablespoon honey

- 2 tablespoon butter

- Salt to taste

- 2 tablespoon shredded coconut

Directions:

1. Take a mixing bowl, add almond flour, coconut flour, cinnamon powder, shredded coconut, salt, honey and mix it together.

2. Set the sous vide machine to 145 degrees Fahrenheit.

3. Take the dates, cut them in half and discard the pit. Place them in a ziplock bag. Remove air and seal.

4. Submerge this bag in water bath and heat for 8 minutes.

5.   Make a thick paste of dates and add it to the flour mixture and mix properly.

6.   Add the almond milk to the mixture and

stir continuously to make a smooth batter.

7.   Heat a non-stick pan and add a small amount of butter. Fry the pancakes till they turn golden brown.

8.   Serve them hot with a drizzle of honey.

Nutrition: calories 110kcal.

Cup Cake With Coffee

Preparation time: 15 minutes Cooking time: 35 minutes Servings: 12

Ingredients:

- 1/2 cup brown sugar
- 1/4 cup softened butter
- 1 cup oatmeal
- 1 teaspoon cinnamon powder
- 2 eggs
- 1 cup sugar
- 2 cups all-purpose flour
- 1 cup milk
- 1/4 cup vegetable oil
- 1 teaspoon vanilla
- 2 teaspoon baking powder
- 1/2 teaspoon baking soda
- 1/8 teaspoon nutmeg powder
- 1/4 spoon salt

Directions:

1.   Take a large mixing bowl, crack 2 large eggs and beat it with fork or wire until it is completely blended together. Add milk and mix it properly to make a smooth mixture.

2.   Add oil, sugar and vanilla and again mix thoroughly.

3.   Take another bowl and sift all the dry powder like flour, baking powder, baking soda, salt, nutmeg together and mix them well. Add all this dry mixture to the egg and milk mixture. Mix it with the spoon till everything is uniformly combined.

4.   Take a baking pan and grease it with unsalted butter or cooking spray. Set this tray side.

5.   For the streusel, take a mixing bowl and

add brown sugar, butter and cinnamon powder till it is properly mixed. Add oatmeal to this mixture and mix till it becomes crumbly.

6.   Set the sous vide machine to 195 degrees Fahrenheit.

7.   Take small glass jars for making the cupcakes. Put the cake batter in the jars; sprinkle the oatmeal streusel evenly over the cake batter. Seal the bottles.

8.   Place the bottles in the water bath for 30 minutes.

9.   Let it cool for 15 minutes, and serve.

Nutrition: calories 189kcal per slice.

Scrambled Eggs

Preparation time: 15 minutes Cooking time: 30 minutes Servings: 8

Ingredients:

- 12 eggs

- 1/2 cup heavy cream

- 2 tablespoon butter

- 1 cup sour cream

- 1 cup shredded cheddar cheese

- 1/8 teaspoon white pepper

- 1/2 teaspoon salt

Directions:

1.   Take a large skillet and melt butter. Add the egg mixture to the skillet and cook it at low flame. Stir the mixture frequently until the eggs are set.

2.   Remove the pan from the heat and add the sour cream. Mix it properly.

3.   Take a glass vessel. Add the egg and cream mixture to it. Sprinkle the shredded cheese over it evenly and set aside for some time. Sprinkle with pepper and salt and lightly mix. Cover the vessel and seal.

4.   Set the sous vide machine to 195 degrees Fahrenheit.

5.   Place this vessel in the water bath and heat for 30 minutes.

6.   Serve hot.

Nutrition: calories 180kcal.

Bread with Cranberry

Preparation time: 10 minutes Cooking time: 30 minutes Servings: 12

Ingredients:

- 1 1/2 cup all-purpose flour

- 1/2 cup sugar

- 6 tablespoons unsalted butter

- 1 egg

- 3/4 cup milk

- 1/2 cup sour cream

- 1/4 cup orange juice

- 4 tablespoons orange zest

- 1/4 teaspoon vanilla extract

- 1 cup fresh cranberries

- 1/4 teaspoon salt

- 1 cup powdered sugar

- 2 1/2 teaspoons baking powder

Directions:

1. Take a large mixing bowl. Sift all the dry ingredients which include the all-purpose flour, sugar, salt, baking powder and mix well.

2.   Melt the butter and bring it to room temperature.

3.   Take another mixing bowl and beat the egg. Add milk, sour cream, orange juice, vanilla, orange zest, melted butter to the egg while continuous mixing.

4.   In the bowl containing the dry ingredients, make a well in the center and add all above wet mixture while continuous stirring.

5.   Mix the ingredients thoroughly until the mixture is uniformly combined. Add cranberries to this mixture and mix properly.

6.   Allow it to sit for some time, the mixture thickens.

7.   Set the sous vide machine to 195 degrees Fahrenheit.

8.   Take the above dough in the sous vide bag and seal it by removing all the air.

9.   Place the bag in sous vide and cook for 30 minutes.

10.   Remove it, allow it to cool.

11.   Sprinkle some powdered sugar on the surface of the bread loaf. Spread some orange juice on the loaf.

12.   Cut it into slices and serve.

Nutrition: calories 310kcal.

Muffins with Blueberry

Preparation time: 5 minutes Cooking time: 12 hours Servings: 12

Ingredients:

*   1 1/3 cup all-purpose flour

*   1 egg

*   3/4 cup whole milk

*   1/2 cup sour cream

*   6 tablespoons unsalted butter

*   1/4 cup sugar

*   2 1/2 teaspoons baking powder

*   1/4 teaspoon salt

*   1 cup fresh blueberries

Directions:

1.   Take a large mixing bowl. Combine all the dry ingredients which include the all- purpose flour, baking powder, sugar and salt.

2.   Melt the unsalted butter and bring it to room temperature.

3.   Take a mixing bowl. Beat the egg till it is properly whisked. Add milk, sour cream, vanilla and melted butter to the whisked egg with continuous stirring. Mix well so that all the ingredients are uniformly mixed with no lump formation.

4.   In the bowl containing the dry ingredients, add this egg and milk mixture gradually with continuous stirring. Do not over mix the contents.

5.   Add blueberries to the batter and allow it to rest. The batter thickens after a short period.

6.   Set the sous vide machine to 115 degrees Fahrenheit.

7.   Take small glass jars to make the muffins.

Place the muffin paper cups in to the jar and add the batter or directly add batter into these jars and seal the jar properly.

8.   Place this jars in water bath and cook for 12 hours.

9.   If directly adding batter to the jars make use of a knife to remove the muffins from the jars. If using paper cups remove them and serve warm.

Nutrition: calories 313kcal per muffin.

Omelet with pasta and cheese

Preparation time: 10 minutes Cooking time: 15 minutes Servings: 4

Ingredients:

- 1/2 cup chopped green pepper

- 1/2 cup chopped onion

- 6 eggs

- 1 tablespoon butter

- 2 tablespoons olive oil

- 1/4 cup milk

- 1/2 teaspoon dried basil leaves

- 1/3 cup + 1/4 grated Parmesan cheese

- 1/4 cup shredded Muenster cheese

- 1 cup cooked spaghetti

- Pepper and salt

Directions:

1. Cook the spaghetti and cut into 2" pieces.

2. Heat the skillet over medium heat. Heat olive oil and butter until it melts and becomes foamy.

3. Add the onion and bell peppers with continuous stirring till it turns crisp- tender.

4. Take a large mixing bowl. Beat the eggs and add milk to it. Add salt, pepper, basil and 1/3 cup Parmesan cheese to the above egg mixture.

5. Add the cooked spaghetti to the egg mixture and mix lightly.

6. Take a glass vessel and add the mixture of egg and spaghetti arranging it in even layers.

7. Spread the Muenster cheese and 1/4 cup Parmesan cheese evenly on its surface.

8. Close the lid and remove all the air to seal.

9. Set the sous vide machine to 175 degrees Fahrenheit.

10. Place the vessel in the sous vide machine and cook for 5-10 minutes.

11. Cut the pasta omelet into wedges and serve hot.

Nutrition: calories 280kcal.

Bread with tasty bananas

Preparation time: 25 minutes Cooking time: 60 minutes Servings: 10

Ingredients:

- 1 cup mashed ripe banana

- 1 egg

- 1/2 cup sugar

- 1/4 cup brown sugar

- 1/2 cup unsalted butter

- 2 cups all-purpose flour

- 2 teaspoons vanilla

- 2 teaspoons baking powder

- 1/2 teaspoon baking soda

- 3 tablespoons buttermilk

- 1 teaspoon cinnamon powder

- 2 tablespoons powdered sugar

- 1/4 teaspoon salt

Directions:

1.   Whip butter, sugar and brown sugar together till it becomes light and fluffy. Add egg, vanilla to this mixture and beat well.

2.   Take a mixing bowl. Sift the dry ingredients like all-purpose flour, baking powder, cinnamon, baking powder, baking soda and salt. Mix all these dry ingredients well.

3.   Take another mixing bowl. In this, mix banana with buttermilk.

4.   Take the butter mixture. Add the small amount of dry ingredients and banana mixture alternately with continuous stirring. It should form a uniform and smooth batter.

5.   Set the sous vide machine to 195 degrees Fahrenheit.

6.   Take the above dough in the sous vide bag.

7.   In a small bowl, combine cinnamon powder and the powdered sugar.

8.   Sprinkle this sugar cinnamon mixture over the batter.

9.   Seal the bag by removing all the air and place the bag in sous vide and cook for 45 minutes.

10.   Remove the bread from the bag and allow it to cool and serve.

Nutrition: calories 158kcal per slice.

Swiss Eggs

Preparation time: 15 minutes Cooking time: 45 minutes Servings: 8

Ingredients:

- 1 pound pork sausage

- 12 eggs

- 2 cups shredded Swiss cheese

- 2 tablespoons mustard

- 1/2 cup light cream

- 1/8 teaspoon pepper

Directions:

1. Take a saucepan. Break the meat using a fork and cook it on a medium flame till it turns brown.

2. Grease the baking dish with butter or cooking spray. Fill this cooked sausage in this baking dish and spread shredded cheese over it.

3. Take a small mixing bowl. Mix the pepper, mustard and cream thoroughly to make a smooth paste.

4. Add this smooth paste over the sausage and cheese.

5. Take another mixing bowl and beat eggs in it till it becomes frothy. Pour these eggs in the baking dish over the cream mixture. Add some butter on the frothy eggs.

6.   Set the sous vide machine to 195 degrees Fahrenheit.

7.   Take the above mixture is a glass vessel. Remove the air and seal.

8.   Place the vessel in sous vide and cook for 40 minutes.

9.   Cut it into square pieces and serve.

Nutrition: calories 380kcal.

Sandwich with Salmon

Preparation time: 10 minutes Cooking time: 20 minutes Servings: 8

Ingredients:

- 16 Brown bread slices
- 5-6 ounce salmon fillets
- 2/3 cup low-fat mayonnaise
- 1/3 cup grated Parmesan cheese
- 3 tablespoons honey mustard
- 1 orange bell pepper
- 1 red bell pepper
- 3 stalks celery
- 1/2 teaspoon marjoram
- Salt and pepper to taste

Directions:

1. Cut the salmon into small pieces.

2. Chop the bell peppers and celery stalks.

3. Take a large mixing bowl. Add mayonnaise, cheese, honey mustard, and mix well.

4. Set the sous vide machine to 175 degrees Fahrenheit.

5.   Take the salmon fillets in the ziplock bags, sprinkle some salt and pepper. Seal the bag to remove the air.

6.   Place the bag in sous vide and cook for 20 minutes.

7.   Add these cooked salmon pieces and chopped vegetables and mix.

8.   Add the marjoram, salt and pepper and toss to mix evenly.

9.   Chill the sandwich spread.

10.   Apply the spread on the bread and serve.

Nutrition: calories 290kcal per sandwich..

Fish and Seafood

Recipes

Haddock On Vegetable Sauce

Preparation time: 10 minutes

Cooking time: 30 minutes fish, 40 minutes vegetables

Servings: 4

Ingredients:

- 4 6oz.. haddock fillets

Marinade:

- 1 pinch curry
- 1 pinch brown sugar
- 1 pinch fine sea salt
- 5 tablespoons olive oil
- 1 sprig thyme, chopped
- 1 teaspoon lemon juice

Vegetables:

- 1 pinch chili powder
- 1 cucumber
- 3 carrots
- 1 leek, chopped
- 1 tablespoon olive oil
- 3 bell peppers, red, yellow, and green
- 1 sweet potato
- Salt, and pepper, to taste

Directions:

1. Preheat Sous Vide cooker to 130F.

2. In a Sous Vide bag combine marinade ingredients.

3.   Add haddock fillets and shake to coat the fish.

4.   Vacuum seal the bag and cook 30 minutes.

5.   In a separate Sous Vide bag, combine all vegetables, with seasonings, and olive oil. Vacuum seal the bag and cook the veggies in Sous Vide at 185F 40 minutes.

Finishing steps:

1.   Open the bags carefully.

2.   Heat some olive oil in a large skillet. Cook

the fish fillets 2 minutes per side.

3.   Serve fish with vegetables.

Nutrition:

Calories 349 Total Fat 19g Total Carb 22g Dietary Fiber 2g Protein 27g

Lobster Risotto

Preparation time: 40 minutes Cooking time: 1 hourServings: 2

Ingredients:

- 1 lobster, claws and tail separated from the carapace
- 1 carrot, coarsely chopped
- 1 stalk celery, coarsely chopped
- 1 onion, coarsely chopped
- 2 cloves garlic
- 2 sprigs thyme
- 1 bay leaf
- 1 teaspoon salt
- 1 teaspoon pepper
- 2 tablespoons white wine
- ¼ cup butter
- 1 cup arborio rice
- ¼ cup grated Parmesan

Directions:

1. Preheat the water bath to 140°F. Seal lobster tail and claws into a bag. Place in water bath and cook 1 hour. Transfer to an ice bath once cooked.

2. While the lobster is cooking, make the stock. Place the carapace in a pot with the carrot, celery, onion, garlic, thyme, bay leaf, and salt and pepper. Add about 6 cups water. Bring to a boil and simmer 1 hour. Liquid should reduce by half. Strain solids. Stir in wine.

3. When the stock is finished, make the risotto. Melt the butter in a pot. Add rice and toast for about 2 minutes. Pour in ¼ cup of stock. Stir until the liquid is mostly

absorbed. Continue adding the stock ¼ cup at a time until you have added 3 cups of stock.

4.Shell lobster and chop into bite-size pieces. Stir into risotto along with Parmesan and pepper to taste. Serve.

Nutrition:

Calories 754 Total Fat 285g Total Carb 985g Dietary Fiber 5g Protein 259g

San Francisco Cioppino

Preparation time: 30 minutes Cooking time: 1 hour Servings: 2

Ingredients:

- 1 pound shrimp, shelled
- 1 pound clams, scrubbed
- 1 pound scallops, trimmed if necessary
- 1 pound halibut fillet, cut into 1-inch pieces
- 1 tablespoon olive oil
- 1 onion, chopped
- 1 stalk celery, chopped
- 4 cloves garlic, minced
- 1 can (28 ounces whole tomatoes, crushed
- 1 cup clam juice
- 1 cup chicken broth
- 1 cup white wine
- ¼ cup fresh basil, chopped
- ¼ cup fresh parsley, chopped
- Crusty bread, preferably sourdough, for serving

Directions:

1.   Preheat the water bath to 140°F. Seal shrimp, clams, scallops, and halibut into separate bags and place in water bath. Remove scallops and clams after 20 minutes and halibut and shrimp after 45 minutes.

2.   Meanwhile, prepare the soup. Heat olive

oil in the pan. Add onion and celery and cook until onion is translucent, then add garlic. Add tomatoes, clam juice, chicken broth, white wine, and bay leaf and cook until reduced by ⅓. Stir in basil, parsley, and seafood until heated through. Serve with crusty bread.

Nutrition: Calories 619 Total Fat 275g Total Carb 268g Dietary Fiber 9g Protein 726g

Linguine with Clam Sauce

Preparation time: 20 minutes Cooking time: 20 minutes Servings: 2

Ingredients:

- 2 dozen clams, cleaned
- 2 tablespoons butter
- 1 tablespoon flour
- 3 garlic cloves, minced
- ¼ cup white wine
- 1 teaspoon pepper
- ¼ cup fresh basil, chopped
- Cooked linguine for serving

Directions:

1. Preheat the water bath to 180°F.

2. Seal clams into the bag. Place in water bath and cook 15 minutes.

3. Meanwhile, prepare the sauce. Melt butter in a pan. Add garlic and stir. Add flour and cook until bubbling subsides. Pour in wine, stirring rapidly, until sauce thickens. When clams are cooked, add to sauce along with cooking liquid. Stir in basil.

4. Serve clam sauce on top of cooked linguine.

Nutrition: Calories 292 Total Fat 132g Total Carb 117g Dietary Fiber 6g

Protein 259g

Lazy Man's Lobster

Preparation time: 20 minutes Cooking time: 1 hour Servings: 1

Ingredients:

- Tail and claws of 1 lobster
- 2 tablespoons butter
- 1 clove garlic, minced
- ½ tablespoon fresh thyme, minced
- ¼ cup sherry
- ½ teaspoon salt
- ½ teaspoon pepper
- ¼ cup heavy cream
- Toast for serving

Directions:

1.   Preheat the water bath to 140°F. Seal lobster into the bag. Place in water bath and cook 1 hour.

2.   Meanwhile, prepare the sauce. Melt butter in a pan. Add garlic and thyme and cook 30 seconds. Add sherry and bring to a boil. Remove from heat and stir in cream. Season with salt and pepper.

3.   When lobster is cooked, remove the shell and stir into sauce. Serve with toast.

Nutrition:

Calories 582 Total Fat 426g Total Carb 45g Dietary Fiber 6g Protein 27g

Whole Red Snapper

Preparation time: 20 minutes Cooking time: 1 hour Servings: 2

Ingredients:

- 1 small red snapper, cleaned and gutted
- 1 teaspoon salt
- 1 teaspoon pepper
- 4 garlic cloves, crushed

- 2 sprigs rosemary
- 1 lemon, cut into wedges
- 2 tablespoons butter, cut into pats

Directions:

1.   Preheat the water bath to 140°F.

2.   Season the fish all over with salt and pepper. Stuff the center of the fish with garlic, rosemary, half the lemon, and butter.

3.   Seal into a bag and place in water bath. Cook 60 minutes. Serve with remaining lemon wedges.

Nutrition:

Calories 800 Total Fat 277g Total Carb 58g Dietary Fiber 6g Protein 1429g

Teriyaki Salmon

Preparation time: 10 minutes Cooking time: 15 minutes Servings: 2

Ingredients:

- ½ cup plus 1 teaspoon teriyaki sauce
- 2 (5 oz. skinless salmon fillets
- 4 oz. Chinese egg noodles
- 1 tablespoon sesame oil
- 2 teaspoons soy sauce
- 2 teaspoons thinly sliced scallions,

  plus 4 (1-inch pieces scallion greens, for serving
- 1-inch fresh ginger, peeled and sliced into thin

  strips
- 4 oz. lettuce, chopped
- 1/8 small red onion, thinly sliced
- 1 tablespoon Japanese roasted sesame dressing
- 1 tablespoon sesame seeds, toasted

Directions:

1. Divide ½ cup teriyaki sauce between 2 zip-lock bags.

2. Place 1 salmon fillet in each bag and seal bags using water immersion method.

3. Do not place salmon fillets, but place aside to marinate at room temperature for 15 minutes.

4. Meanwhile, set the Sous Vide precision cooker to 131F.

5. Place the bags in a water bath and cook for 15 minutes.

6. While salmon is cooking, prepare egg noodles according to package instructions.

7.   Drain well, return to cooking pot and stir in sesame oil and soy sauce, reserving one teaspoon

8.   Divide pasta between serving plates.

9.   Prepare the dipping sauce; combine scallions, ginger, remaining teriyaki sauce and one teaspoon soy sauce.

10.   Also, prepare the salad by combining lettuce and onion with one tablespoon roasted sesame dressing.

Finishing steps:

1.   When the timer goes off, remove salmon from the water bath, reserving cooking liquid.

2.   Top the pasta with salmon fillets and drizzle all with reserved cooking liquid.

3.   Garnish salmon with sesame seeds and serve with prepared salad and dipping sauce.

Nutrition:

Calories 291 Total Fat 12g Total Carb 12g Dietary Fiber 2g Protein 33g

Crusted Tuna Fish

Preparation time: 10 minutes Cooking time: 25 minutes Servings: 4

Ingredients:

- 3 tablespoons all-purpose flour
- 3 tablespoons ground almonds
- ½ tablespoon butter
- 4 5oz. tuna fillets

Marinade:

- 1 pinch chili powder
- 1 pinch salt
- 1 pinch black pepper
- 5 tablespoons vegetable oil
- 2 teaspoons lemon juice

Directions:

1. Preheat Sous Vide cooker to 132F.

2. Combine the marinade ingredients in a Sous Vide bag.

3. Add the tuna and vacuum seal.

4. Submerge in a water bath and cook 25 minutes.

Finishing steps:

1. Remove the fish from Sous vide bag. Pat dry the fish.

2. In a bowl, combine all-purpose flour and almonds. Sprinkle with a pinch of salt.

3. Heat the butter in a large skillet.

4. Coat the tuna with the flour-nut mixture and fry in butter until golden brown.

5.   Serve warm.

Nutrition:

Calories 324 Total Fat 12g Total Carb 4g Dietary Fiber 7g Protein 32g

Crab Zucchini Roulade with Mousse

Preparation time: 30 minutes + inactive time Cooking time: 10 minutes

Servings: 4

Ingredients:

- 3lb. crab legs and claws
- 2 tablespoons olive oil
- 1 medium zucchini
- Salt and pepper, to taste

Mousse:

- 1 avocado, peeled, pitted
- 1 tablespoon Worcestershire sauce
- 2 tablespoons crème Fraiche
- 2 tablespoons fresh lime juice
- Salt, to taste

Directions:

1. Preheat Sous vide cooker to 185F.

2. Place the claws and legs in a Sous Vide bag and vacuum seal.

3. Submerge the bag with content in a water bath. Cook the crab 10 minutes.

Finishing steps:

1. Slice the zucchini with a vegetable peeler. This way you will have some skinny strips.

2. Remove the crab from the water bath and crack the shell.

3. Flake the meat and transfer into a bowl. Add olive oil, salt, and pepper, and stir to bind gently.

4.   Make the mousse; in a food blender, blend the avocado and crème Fraiche until smooth.

5.   Stir in the remaining ingredients and spoon the mixture into piping bag.

6.   Arrange the zucchini slices on aluminum foil and fill with the crab meat.

7.   Roll up the zucchinis and crab into a log and refrigerate 30 minutes.

8.   To serve; cut the roulade into four pieces. Serve onto a plate with some avocado mousse.

9.   Enjoy.

Nutrition:

Calories 415 Total Fat 11g Total Carb 6g Dietary Fiber 5g Protein 43g

Coriander-Garlic Squids

Preparation time: 20 minutes Cooking time: 2 hours Servings: 4

Ingredients:

- 4 4oz. squids, cleaned
- ¼ cup olive oil
- ¼ cup chopped coriander
- 4 cloves garlic, minced
- 2 chili pepper, chopped
- 2 teaspoons minced ginger
- ¼ cup vegetable oil
- 1 lemon, cut into wedges
- Salt and pepper, to taste

Method:

1. Set the Sous vide cooker to 136F.

2. Place the squids and 2 tablespoons olive oil in a Sous Vide bags. Season to taste and vacuum seal the bag.

3. Submerge in water and cook 2 hours.

Finishing steps:

1. Heat remaining olive oil in a skillet. Add garlic, chili pepper, and ginger and cook 1 minute. Add half the coriander and stir well. Remove from the heat.

2. Remove the squids from the bag.

3. Heat vegetable oil in a skillet, until sizzling hot. Add the squid and cook 30 seconds per side.

4. Transfer the squids onto a plate. Top with garlic-coriander mixture and sprinkle with the remaining coriander.

5. Serve with lemon.

Nutrition: Calories 346 Total Fat 29g Total Carb 7g Dietary Fiber 7g Protein 12g

Poultry Recipes

Chicken Breast With Mushroom Sauce

Preparation Time: 15 minutes Cooking Time: 4 hours Cooking Temperature: 140°F Ingredients:

For Chicken:

- 2 boneless, skinless chicken breasts
- ⅛ teaspoon salt
- 1 teaspoon vegetable oil

For Mushroom Sauce:

- 1 teaspoon olive oil
- 3 French shallots, finely chopped
- 2 tablespoons butter
- 2 large garlic cloves, finely chopped
- 1 cup button mushrooms, sliced
- 2 tablespoons port wine
- ½ cup chicken broth
- 1 cup cream
- Salt, to taste
- ¼ teaspoon cracked black pepper

Directions:

1. Attach the sous vide immersion circulator to a Cambro container or pot with water using an adjustable clamp and preheat water to 140°F.

2. Season chicken breasts lightly with salt.

3. Place chicken breasts in a large cooking pouch. Seal pouch tightly after removing the excess air. Place pouch in sous vide bath and set the cooking time for 1½-4 hours.

4. For the mushroom sauce: heat olive oil in a skillet over medium heat and sauté shallots for 2-3 minutes. Stir in butter and garlic and sauté for 1 minute.

5.	Increase the heat to medium-high. Stir in mushrooms and cook until all liquid is absorbed.

6.	Add wine. Cook until all liquid is absorbed then add broth and cook for 2 minutes.

7.	Stir in cream and reduce heat back to medium. Once the sauce becomes thick, stir in the black pepper and desired amount of salt and remove from heat.

8.	Remove pouch from the sous vide bath and open carefully. Remove chicken breasts from pouch and pat dry chicken breasts completely with paper towels. Coat chicken breasts evenly with vegetable oil.

9.	Heat a grill pan over high heat and cook chicken breasts for 1 minute per side.

10.	Divide onto serving plates once cooked, top with mushroom sauce, and serve.

Coq Au Vin

Preparation Time: 20 minutes Cooking Time: 12 hours 30 minutes Cooking Temperature: 151°F Ingredients:

- 1 bottle red wine, reserving 1 glass
- 1/2 cup bacon, crumbled
- 3 large carrots, peeled and chopped
- 3 celery stalks, finely chopped
- 4 garlic cloves, pressed
- 4 bay leaves
- 7 tbsp unsalted butter, divided
- 10 shallots or small onions
- 1 chicken, jointed into 2 breasts on the bone with wings and 2 legs attached
- Sea salt and freshly ground black pepper, to taste
- A few thyme sprigs
- 2 tablespoons all-purpose flour
- Vegetable oil*
- 7 ounces button mushrooms
- Finely chopped fresh parsley, for garnishing

Directions:

1.   Add wine, bacon, carrots, celery, garlic, and bay leaves to a pan and bring to a gentle boil. Cook for 25 minutes, stirring occasionally. Remove from heat and allow to cool completely.

2.   Meanwhile in another pan, melt 1 tbsp butter and sauté onions for 4-5 minutes. Remove from heat and set aside.

3.   Attach the sous vide immersion circulator to a Cambro container or pot with water using an adjustable clamp and preheat water to 151°F.

4.   Season the jointed chickens evenly with salt and black pepper.

5.   Divide chicken pieces, sautéed onions, and thyme sprigs between two cooking pouches. Seal pouches tightly after removing excess air. Place pouches in sous vide bath and set the cooking time for 12 hours.

6.   Preheat the oven to 355°F.

7.   Remove pouches from the sous vide bath and open carefully. Remove chicken pieces from pouches, reserving cooking liquid in a pan. Pat dry chicken pieces with paper towels.

8.   Season chicken lightly with salt and pepper.

9.   In a large frying pan, heat oil and 2 tablespoons butter. Add chicken, skin side down, and fry for 6-8 minutes on each side.

10.   Move chicken pieces to a baking sheet, skin side up, and bake for 10 minutes.

11.   While the chicken is baking, remove thyme sprigs from cooking liquid and bring liquid to a gentle boil, adding reserved wine.

12.   In a bowl, combine flour and 2 tablespoons unsalted butter and mix well. Add flour mixture to pan with cooking liquid, stirring continuously. Stir in salt and black pepper and simmer until desired consistency is reached.

13.   Move baked chicken pieces to a different pan on the stove. Add 2 tablespoons of butter and stir fry with mushrooms for 6-7 minutes or until browned on both sides.

14.   Place chicken on a serving platter and top with sauce, followed by mushrooms. Garnish with parsley and serve.

Simple Chicken Breast

Preparation Time: 10 minutes Cooking Time: 4 hours Cooking Temperature: 146°F

Ingredients:

- 1 chicken breast

- Salt and freshly ground black pepper, to taste

- 1 teaspoon olive oil

Directions:

1.   Attach the sous vide immersion circulator to a Cambro container or pot with water using an adjustable clamp and preheat water to 146°F.

2.   Season chicken breasts lightly with salt and black pepper.

3.   Place chicken breasts in a cooking pouch. Seal pouch tightly after removing the excess air. Place pouch in sous vide bath and set the cooking time for 1-4 hours.

4.   Remove pouch from the sous vide bath and open carefully. Remove chicken breasts from pouch and set aside for 10- 15 minutes to cool. Cut into desired sizes pieces and serve.

Orange Balsamic Chicken

Preparation Time: 15 minutes Cooking Time: 1 hour 35 minutes
Cooking Temperature: 146°F

Ingredients:

*   1 large, whole, boneless chicken breast

*   Salt and freshly ground black pepper, to taste

*   1 orange

*   1 small sprig fresh oregano or rosemary

*   3 tablespoons balsamic vinegar

Directions:

1. Attach the sous vide immersion circulator to a Cambro
container or pot with water using an adjustable clamp and preheat
water to 146°F.

2. Season chicken breasts lightly with salt and black pepper.
Cut 2 (¼-inch slices from orange. Extract juice from remaining
orange into a small bowl. Add vinegar and mix together with the
juice of the orange.

3. Place chicken breast in a cooking pouch and top breast
with orange slices and herb sprig. Carefully pour vinegar mixture
into pouch. Seal pouch tightly after removing the excess air. Place
pouch in sous vide bath and set the cooking time for 1½ hours.

4. Remove pouch from the sous vide bath and open carefully.
Remove chicken breast from the pouch, reserving the cooking
liquid.

5. Add the cooking liquid to a small pan and cook until
slightly thickened.

6. Serve chicken with sauce.

Chicken Parmigiana

Preparation Time: 20 minutes Cooking Time: 12 hours Cooking Temperature: 141°F

Ingredients:

For Chicken:

- 4 chicken breasts
- ½ teaspoon garlic powder
- Salt and freshly ground black pepper, to taste
- 4 fresh rosemary sprigs
- 4 fresh thyme sprigs

For Coating:

- ¾ cup flour
- 2 teaspoons salt
- 1 teaspoon ground black pepper
- 2 eggs
- ¼ cup Parmesan cheese, grated
- ¾ cup dried Italian breadcrumbs
- 2 tablespoons fresh parsley, chopped

For Cooking:

- Oil, as required
- For Topping:
- ½ cup fresh basil, chopped
- 1 cup fresh mozzarella cheese, shredded
- ¼ cup Parmesan cheese, grated

Directions:

1.   Season chicken breasts with garlic powder, salt, and black pepper evenly.

2.   Divide chicken breasts and herb sprigs into two cooking pouches. Seal pouches tightly after removing the excess air. Refrigerate pouches for up to 2 days.

3.   Attach the sous vide immersion circulator to a Cambro container or pot with water using an adjustable clamp and preheat water to 141°F.

4.   Place pouches in sous vide bath and set the cooking time for 2-12 hours.

5.   Preheat the oven broiler.

6.   Remove the pouches from the sous vide bath and open carefully. Remove the chicken breasts and pat dry chicken breasts completely with paper towels.

7.   In a shallow dish, mix together flour, salt, and black pepper for coating. In a second shallow dish, beat eggs. In a third shallow dish, mix together Parmesan cheese, breadcrumbs, and parsley.

8.   Coat chicken breasts evenly with flour mixture, then dip in egg mixture before coating with parmesan mixture.

9.   In a deep skillet, heat ½-inch of oil to 350°F and sear chicken breasts until crust is golden brown then turn and repeat on other side.

10.   Transfer chicken breasts to a sheet pan. Top each breast with the basil, Parmesan, and mozzarella cheese for topping. Broil until cheese is bubbly.

11.   Serve immediately.

Chicken Tikka

Preparation Time: 15 minutes Cooking Time: 2 hours

CookingTemperature: 146°F

Ingredients:

- 4 boneless, skinless chicken breasts
- Salt and freshly ground black pepper, to taste
- 2 tablespoons butter
- 2 cups half-and-half
- 2 cups canned crushed tomatoes
- 4 garlic cloves, peeled
- 1 (1-inch piece fresh ginger, cut into chunks
- 1½ tablespoons honey
- 1 tablespoon ground turmeric
- 1 tablespoon paprika
- 1 tablespoon ground cumin
- 2 teaspoons ground coriander
- ½ teaspoons salt
- 2 cups cooked rice
- Chopped fresh cilantro, for garnishing

Directions:

1. Attach the sous vide immersion circulator to a Cambro container or pot with water using an adjustable clamp and preheat water to 146°F.

2. Season chicken breasts evenly with salt and black pepper.

3. In a food processor, add half-and-half, tomatoes, garlic, ginger, honey, and spices and pulse until smooth.

4. Divide chicken and butter into two cooking pouches with

two chicken breasts and one tablespoon butter in each pouch. Add mixture from food processor into a third, large pouch.

Seal pouches tightly after removing the excess air. Place all pouches inthe sous vide bath and set the cooking time for 2 hours.

5.   Remove the pouches from the sous vide bath and open carefully. Remove chicken breasts from pouches and cut into slices of the desired size.

6.   Divide cooked rice onto serving plates. Top with chicken slices and drizzle with sauce. Garnish with cilantro and serve.

Bbq Chicken Breasts

Preparation Time: 15 minutes

Cooking Time: 2 hours 30 minutes Cooking Temperature: 165°F
Ingredients:

For BBQ Sauce:

- 3 dried ancho chile peppers, stemmed and seeded
- 1 dried New Mexico chile pepper, stemmed and seeded
- ¼ cup sunflower oil
- 1 small yellow onion, chopped
- 2 garlic cloves, minced
- 4½ ounces tomato paste
- ½ cup apple cider vinegar
- ¼ cup brown sugar
- ¼ cup molasses
- 3 tablespoons cocoa powder
- 1½ teaspoons ground cumin
- 1 teaspoon ground coriander
- 1 tablespoon sea salt
- 2 teaspoons ground black pepper
- 1 teaspoon fresh lemon zest, grated
- ¼ cup fresh lemon juice
- ¼ cup fresh lime juice, divided
- 1 teaspoon fresh lime zest, grated

For Chicken:

- 4 skin-on, bone-in chicken breasts
- Sea salt and freshly ground black pepper, to taste

For Garnishing:

- 1 orange, cut into 8 wedges

- Fresh cilantro, chopped

Directions:

1.   In a heatproof bowl, add both types of chile peppers. Add enough hot water to cover and set aside for 15 minutes.

2.   Drain chile peppers, reserving ½ cup of the soaking water. In a blender, add chile peppers and reserved soaking water and pulse until a smooth paste is formed.

3.   Heat oil in a medium pan over medium heat. Add and sauté onion and garlic for 10 minutes.

4.   Add chile paste and remaining BBQ sauce ingredients except for 2 tablespoons of lime juice and the lime zest and bring to a boil. Reduce heat to low and simmer for 20-30 minutes.

5.   Remove from heat and set aside to cool completely. Stir in remaining lime juice and lime zest. Transfer to a container and refrigerate before using.

6.   Attach the sous vide immersion circulator to a Cambro container or pot with water using an adjustable clamp and preheat water to 165°F.

7.   Season chicken breasts evenly with salt and black pepper.

8.   Divide the chicken breasts into two large pouches. Seal pouches tightly after removing the excess air. Place pouches in sous vide bath and set the cooking time for 2½ hours.

9.   Preheat grill to high heat. Grease grill grate.

10.   Remove pouches from the sous vide bath and open carefully. Remove chicken breasts and coat each breast with BBQ sauce. Grill chicken breasts for 1 minute per side.

11.   Serve with orange wedges and cilantro.

Spinach Stuffed Chicken Breasts

Preparation Time: 20 minutes Cooking Time: 1 hour 5 minutes
Cooking Temperature: 145°F Ingredients:

- 2 chicken breasts, pounded thinly

- 2 tablespoons olive oil, divided

- ½ shallot, minced

- 2 garlic cloves, minced

- 2 cups fresh spinach

- 1 teaspoon red pepper flakes, crushed

- Salt and freshly ground black pepper, to taste

- 3 tablespoons heavy cream

- ¼ cup Parmesan cheese, grated

Directions:

1.   Attach the sous vide immersion circulator to a Cambro container or pot with water using an adjustable clamp and preheat water to 145°F.

2.   In a skillet, heat 1 tablespoon of oil and sauté shallot and garlic until fragrant. Stir in spinach, red pepper flakes, salt, and black pepper and cook until spinach is wilted. Add heavy cream and simmer for 1-2 minutes. Remove from the heat and stir in Parmesan cheese. Set aside to cool.

3.   Place half of spinach mixture on one chicken breast and roll chicken from top to bottom. Secure with toothpicks. Repeat with remaining filling and chicken breast. Season both breast rolls with salt and black pepper.

4.   Place chicken rolls in one large cooking pouch. Seal pouch tightly after removing the excess air. Place pouch in sous vide bath and set the cooking time for 1 hour.

5.   Remove pouch from the sous vide bath and open carefully. Remove the chicken rolls from pouch and pat dry the chicken rolls completely with paper towels.

6.   In a large skillet, heat remaining tablespoon of oil and sear chicken rolls until golden brown on both sides.

7.   Remove from skillet, cut each roll into desired slices, and serve.

Chicken Marsala

Preparation Time: 20 minutes Cooking Time: 2 hours 20 minutes Cooking Temperature: 141°F Ingredients:

- 4 chicken breasts

- Salt and freshly ground black pepper, to taste

- 1-2 fresh thyme sprigs

- 1 cup all-purpose flour

- Olive oil, as required

- 3 tablespoons butter, divided

- 3 cups fresh mushrooms (baby bella, cremini, oyster, or porcini, sliced

- ¾ cup Marsala wine

- ¾ cup chicken broth

- 4 tablespoons fresh Italian parsley, chopped

Directions:

1.   Attach the sous vide immersion circulator to a Cambro container or pot with water using an adjustable clamp and preheat water to 141°F.

2.   Season chicken breasts generously with salt and black pepper.

3.   Place chicken breasts in a cooking pouch and add thyme sprigs. Seal pouch tightly after removing the excess air. Place pouch in sous vide bath and set the cooking time for 1½-2 hours.

4.   Remove the pouch from the sous vide bath and open carefully. Remove chicken breasts from pouch and pat dry chicken breasts completely with paper towels. Evenly coat chicken breasts with flour.

5.   In a sauté pan, heat olive oil over high heat and sear chicken breasts for 1 minute per side. Transfer chicken breasts onto a plate and cover with a piece of foil to keep warm.

6.   In the same pan, melt 1 tablespoon of butter over medium-high heat and sauté mushrooms for 4-6 minutes. Reduce heat to medium and stir in wine. Simmer for 1 minute, scraping the browned bits from bottom. Add the chicken broth and simmer for 5-10 minutes. Remove from heat and immediately stir in remaining butter.

7.   Divide chicken breasts onto serving plates. Evenly top with mushroom sauce. Garnish with parsley and serve.

Prosciutto Wrapped Chicken

Preparation Time: 15 minutes Cooking Time: 1 hour 5 minutes
Cooking Temperature: 145°F

Ingredients:

• 2 (6-ounce boneless, skinless chicken breasts, sliced in half lengthwise

• Kosher salt and freshly ground black

pepper, to taste

• 2 thin prosciutto slices

• 1 tablespoon extra-virgin olive oil

Directions:

1. Attach the sous vide immersion circulator to a Cambro container or pot with water using an adjustable clamp and preheat water to 145°F.

2. Season chicken breasts evenly with salt and black pepper.

3. Arrange a piece of plastic wrap onto a cutting board. Place one prosciutto slice in the center of the plastic wrap. Arrange two of the strips of chicken in the center of prosciutto, side-by-side to form an even rectangle. Roll prosciutto around the chicken so that it creates a uniform cylinder. Wrap the cylinder tightly in the plastic wrap and tie off the ends with butcher's twine. Repeat with remaining prosciutto and chicken.

4. Place the chicken cylinders in a large cooking pouch. Seal pouch tightly after removing the excess air. Place the pouch in the sous vide bath and set the cooking time for 1 hour.

5. Remove pouch from the sous vide bath and open carefully. Remove the chicken cylinders from the pouch and take off the plastic wrap, patting dry the chicken cylinders. Season each cylinder with salt and black pepper.

6. In a large, non-stick skillet, heat olive oil over medium-high heat and sear chicken cylinders for 5 minutes or until golden brown.

7.   Remove from heat and allow to cool for 10 minutes. Cut into desired slices and serve.

Hawaiian Chicken

Preparation Time: 15 minutes Cooking Time: 3 hours 5 minutes Cooking Temperature: 147°F Ingredients:

For Glaze:

*   2 cups chicken broth

*   1½ cups soy sauce

*   ¾ cup light brown sugar

*   ½ cup plus 1 tablespoon water, divided

*   ½ cup mirin

*   1 tablespoon fish sauce

*   3 tablespoons cornstarch

*   1 tablespoon water

For Chicken:

*   6 pounds boneless, skinless chicken thighs

*   1 (3-inch piece fresh ginger, peeled and cut into three pieces

*   6 large garlic cloves, minced

For Garnishing:

*   1 cup scallions, thinly sliced

Directions:

1.   Attach the sous vide immersion circulator to a Cambro container or pot with water using an adjustable clamp and preheat water to 147°F.

2.   In a large bowl, add chicken broth, soy sauce, brown sugar, ½ cup water, mirin, and fish sauce and beat until well combined for the glaze.

3.   Divide the glaze, chicken, ginger, and garlic into three cooking pouches. Seal the pouches tightly after removing the excess air. Place pouches in sous vide bath and set the cooking time for 3 hours.

4.   Remove the pouches from the sous vide bath and open carefully. Strain half of the cooking liquid into a pan. Transfer all chicken into a new cooking pouch and seal it. Return pouch to sous vide bath with the sous vide turned off.

5.   Place pan of reserved cooking liquid on stove and bring to a boil. In a small bowl, dissolve cornstarch into 1 tablespoon of water. Add the cornstarch mixture to the cooking liquid, stirring continuously. Cook until the glaze becomes thick.

6.   Place chicken on a platter and top with glaze. Garnish with scallions and serve.

Meat Recipes

Pumpkin Meatballs

Preparation Time: 20 min Cooking Time: 2 h Servings: 6

Ingredients:

- 1/2 cup fresh pumpkin, grated

- 8 pounds minced beef

- 1 garlic clove, minced

- 1 shallot, finely sliced

- 1 big egg

- Salt and pepper to taste

Directions:

1. Preheat your Sous Vide machine to 142 degrees F.

2. In a big bowl, combine the minced beef with the grated pumpkin, egg, garlic, shallot, salt and pepper. Mix well until even.

3. Make 6 meatballs.

4. Carefully put the balls into the vacuum bag.

5. Seal the bag removing the air as much as possible, put it into the water bath and set the cooking time for 2 hours.

6. Serve warm with a preferred sauce.

Nutrition:

Calories: 283

Protein: 30 g

Fats: 13 g

Carbs: 11 g

Veal Cheeks in Red Wine

Preparation Time: 20 min Cooking Time: 8 h 10 min

Servings: 6

Ingredients:

- 4 veal cheeks

- 1 shallot, finely sliced

- 2 celery sticks, diced

- 2 cups meat broth

- 1 carrot, diced

- 1 tsp dried basil

- 2 tbsp liquid honey

- 1 cup tomatoes in own juice, crushed

- 1 tbsp olive oil

- Salt and pepper to taste

Directions:

1. Preheat your Sous Vide machine to 78 degrees F.

2.   Season the cheeks with salt and paper and place them in the vacuum bag.

3.   Heat the olive oil in the saucepan and saute shallot, carrot, celery and garlic for 3 minutes.

4.   Add the red wine and cook until the liquid almost evaporates.

5.   Add the crushed tomatoes and meat broth, and cook until the liquid is reduced by half.

6.   When the sauce cools down, add it to the vacuum bag and seal it, removing the air.

7.   Cook in the preheated water bath for 8 hours.

8.   Serve hot over the baked potato.

Nutrition:

Calories: 350

Protein: 15 g

Fats: 24 g

Carbs: 13 g

Beef Stroganoff

Preparation Time: 20 min Cooking Time: 1 h 20 min

Servings: 2

Ingredients:

- 1 1/2 pounds beef loin

- 6 tbsp unsalted butter

- 1 cup button mushrooms, chopped

- 1 onion, finale chopped

- 3 tbsp all-purpose flour

- 1 cup beef broth

- 2 tbsp dry white wine

- 1 cup sour cream

- Rosemary sprigs

Directions:

1.   Preheat your Sous Vide machine to 136
degrees F.

2.   Season the steaks with salt and paper and place them in the vacuum bag, putting a piece of butter and rosemary sprigs on top of each steak.

3.   Seal the bag and cook the steaks in the preheated water bath for 1 hour.

4.   In the meantime, heat 2 tbsp butter in a skillet and saute the chopped onion until translucent.

5.   Add the mushrooms, salt and pepper to taste, and cook until the liquid evaporates. Set aside.

6.   Sear the steaks in 1 tbsp butter. Set aside.

7.   Add 2 tbsp butter and flour to the pan, mix it well with a spoon, add the stock, wine and cooked mushrooms.

8.   Cook until the sauce thickens. Stir in the sour cream and serve the sauce with the chopped steak over mashed potato.

Nutrition:

Calories: 361

Protein: 35 g

Fats: 16 g

Carbs: 17 g

Beef Bourguignon

Preparation Time: 20 min Cooking Time: 24 h + 1 h Servings: 4

Ingredients:

- 1 1/2 pounds beef chunks

- 2 tbsp cornstarch

- 2 carrots, peeled and chopped

- 1 onion, peeled and sliced

- 2 garlic cloves, minced

- 1 cup water

- 1 tbsp beef stock

- 1 tbsp tomato paste

- 1 tsp dried thyme

- 1 bay leaf

- 4 tbsp unsalted butter

- 1 cup button mushrooms, chopped

- 2 tbsp flour

- 1 bottle dry red wine

Directions:

1.   Season the beef chunks with salt, pepper and cornstarch, tossing it gently to make sure the chunks are evenly coated. Put the chunks in the vacuum bag.

2.   In a large skillet, heat the olive oil and sear the chunks for about 3 minutes until lightly browned. Transfer the beef to the vacuum bag.

3.   Add carrot, garlic and onion to the skillet, add salt to taste and cook for about 10 minutes, stirring occasionally. Add the vegetables to the vacuum bag.

4.   Finally, add a bottle of wine, tomato paste, beef broth and dried thyme to the bag, seal it and cook for 24 hours in the water bath preheated to 140 degrees F.

5.   Heat a large skillet, combine 2 tbsp butter with the flour to form the paste.

6.   Carefully open the bag and add the liquid to the paste, mixing well to avoid lumps. Simmer for about 5 minutes.

7.   Add everything that is left in the bag, mix well with a spatula and serve over mashed potatoes or cauliflower puree.

Nutrition:

Calories: 461

Protein: 34 g

Fats: 17 g

Beef with Penne and Purple Cabbage

Preparation Time: 5 hours 10 minutes

Servings: 6

You're about to cook the best beef roast you've ever tried! Sous vide is one of the best cooking methods to achieve flavors that will blow you away!

Nutrition: 463 Calories; 18g Fat; 28g Carbs; 42g Protein; 3g Sugars

Ingredients

- 2 pounds beef roast
- Salt and black pepper, to taste
- 20 ounces penne, uncooked
- 2 tablespoons butter
- 1 yellow onion, peeled and chopped
- 1 celery stalk, peeled and chopped
- 2 carrots, peeled and thinly sliced
- 1 teaspoon garlic paste
- 2 cups purple cabbage, shredded
- 2 tablespoons tamari sauce

Directions

1. Preheat a sous vide water bath to 158 degrees F.

2.   Season the beef with salt and black pepper to taste.

3.   Add the seasoned beef to a large-sized cooking pouch and seal tightly. Submerge the cooking pouch in the water bath; cookfor 5 hours.

4.   Pat the beef dry with paper towels and reserve.

5.   Cook the penne pasta according to package directions.

6.   In a wok, melt the butter over medium- high heat. Sautéthe onion, celery and carrot until softened.

7.   Add the garlic paste and cabbage and continue sautéing an additional 3 minutes. Add tamari sauce, penne, and reserved beef to the wok.

8.   Stir fry an additional minute and serve in individual bowls.Bon appétit!

Italian-Style Cold Beef Salad

Preparation Time: 10 hours 10 minutes

Servings: 6

A long-simmered blade steak with crispy vegetables, fresh vinaigrette and flavorful Parmigiano-Reggiano is a classic Italian recipe that you must try.

Nutrition: 306 Calories; 12g Fat; 17g Carbs; 33g Protein; 3g Sugars

Ingredients

- 1 ½ pounds beef blade steak

- 1/2 teaspoon sea salt

- 1/4 teaspoon ground black pepper

- 1 red onion, thinly sliced

- 2 Roma tomatoes, sliced

- 2 heads romaine lettuce

- 1 head radicchio, halved, cored and coarsely chopped

- 1 tender celery rib, thinly sliced

- 2 cucumbers, thinly sliced

- 1/4 cup Sicilian olives, pitted and halved

- 2 tablespoons mayonnaise

- 1/4 cup red wine vinegar

- 1 tablespoon olive oil

- Salt and crushed red pepper flakes, to taste

- 1/2 teaspoon dried oregano

- 4 pepperoncini

- 4 ounces Parmigiano-Reggiano cheese, shaved

Directions

1. Preheat a sous vide water bath to 140 degrees F.

2. Season the beef with salt and black pepper.

3. Add the seasoned beef to a large-sized cooking pouch and seal tightly. Submerge the cooking pouch in the water bath; cookfor 10 hours.

4. Pat the beef dry with paper towels and allow it to rest 5 minutes. Then, thinly slice the beef and allow it to cool completely.

5. Transfer the chilled beef to a salad bowl; add the onion, tomatoes, lettuce, radicchio, celery, cucumber, and olives; toss to combine.

6. In a small mixing dish, thoroughly combine the mayo, vinegar, olive oil, salt, red pepper flakes, and oregano. Add the mayo mixture to the salad bowl.

7. Toss again to combine well and serve topped with sliced pepperoncini and shaved Parmigiano-Reggiano cheese. Bon appétit!

Perfect Aromatic Eye Round

Steaks

Preparation Time: 12 hours 10 minutes

Servings: 6

Eye round steak is tough cut of meat so just go nice and slow. Anyway, for a fork-tender texture, opt for a slightly higher temperature, from 156 to 176 degrees F.

If you prefer a cleaner-tasting sear, sear the steaks on the preheated pan without using any oil.

Nutrition: 309 Calories; 13g Fat; 4g Carbs; 45g Protein; 4g Sugars

Ingredients

- 2 ½ pounds eye round steaks

- Sea salt, to taste

- 1/4 teaspoon freshly ground black pepper, or more to taste

- 1/2 teaspoon red pepper flakes, crushed

- 2 tablespoons peanut oil

- 1 tablespoon dried sage, crushed

- 2 sprigs rosemary

- 1 teaspoon dried basil

- 4 garlic cloves, smashed

- 1 yellow onion, chopped

- 2 bell peppers, chopped

Directions

1. Preheat a sous vide water bath to 140 degrees F.

2. Season the beef with salt, black pepper, and red pepper flakes.

3. Add the seasoned beef to a large-sized cooking pouch and seal tightly. Submerge the cooking pouch in the water bath; cook for 12 hours.

4. Next, heat the peanut oil in a pan over medium-high heat. Sear your steaks until browned on all sides; reserve.

5. Then, cook the remaining ingredients in pan drippings until the vegetables are tender and aromatic. Spoon this mixture onto seared steaks and serve. Enjoy!

Must-Serve Beef

Meatballs

Preparation Time: 12 hours

Servings: 4

You can add a few slices of bacon to this recipe. It gives smokiness and richness to your meatballs.

Nutrition: 366 Calories; 15g Fat; 11g Carbs; 37g Protein; 6g Sugars

Ingredients

- 2 tablespoons grapeseed oil

- 1 teaspoon garlic paste

- 2 onions, finely chopped

- 1 teaspoon fresh ginger, grated

- 1 tablespoon cilantro, minced

- 1 teaspoon dried basil

- 1 pound ground chuck

- 1 ½ tablespoons ketchup

- 1 tablespoon oyster sauce

- Salt and ground black pepper, to taste

- 1/2 teaspoon hot paprika

Directions

1. Heat the oil in a frying pan; once hot, cook the garlic, onions, and ginger until softened.

2. Add the sautéed mixture to a mixing bowl. Add the cilantro, basil, beef, ketchup, oyster sauce, salt, black pepper, and hot paprika.

3. Mix until everything is well incorporated. Shape the mixture into small bowls.

4. Preheat a sous vide water bath to 185 degrees F.

5. Add the meatballs to cooking pouches and seal tightly. Submerge the cooking pouches in the water bath; cook for 11 hours 30 minutes.

6. Serve over hot cooked spaghetti and enjoy!

Melt-in-Your-Mouth Steak

Preparation Time: 24 hours 10 minutes

Servings: 6

Sous vide ensures you get moist and tender steak without losing any nutrition and flavor from the meat.

Mound fresh salad on a plate and enjoy!

Nutrition: 306 Calories; 21g Fat; 4g Carbs; 27g Protein; 0g Sugars

Ingredients

- 2 pounds flat iron steak

- Sea salt, to taste

- 1/3 teaspoon freshly ground black pepper

- 1 teaspoon dried marjoram

- 1/2 teaspoon shallot powder

- 2 tablespoons lard, room temperature

- 2 garlic cloves, minced

- 1 (1-inch piece ginger, grated

Directions

1. Preheat a sous vide water bath to 140 degrees F.

2. Season the steak with salt and black pepper.

3.   Add the seasoned steak to cooking pouches; add the marjoram and shallot powder and seal tightly. Submerge the cooking pouches in the water bath; cook for 24 hours.

4.   Pat the beef dry with paper towels and allow it to rest for 5 minutes.

5.   In a pan, melt the lard over medium-high heat. Now, brown the steak for 2 minutes per side.

6.   Add the garlic and ginger. Cook an additional 2 minutes or until heated through. Bon appétit!

Favorite Cheesy Meatloaf

Preparation Time: 2 hours 40 minutes

Servings: 6

If you're looking for a classic meatloaf recipe that is easy to make, look no further! This meatloaf is great with creamy, rich salad.

Nutrition: 437 Calories; 24g Fat; 19g Carbs; 46g Protein; 2g Sugars

Ingredients

- 1 ½ pounds ground chuck

- 1/2 pound pork, ground

- 1 white onion, finely chopped

- 2 garlic cloves, finely chopped

- 1 jalapeno pepper, minced

- 1/2 teaspoon dried rosemary

- 1 teaspoon dried marjoram

- 1/2 teaspoon dried oregano

- 2 eggs, beaten

- 1 cup rolled oats

- 4 ounces Romano cheese, freshly grated

- Salt and black pepper, to taste

- 3/4 cup tomato puree

- 2 tablespoons brown sugar

- 1 tablespoon grainy mustard

Directions

1.   Preheat a sous vide water bath to 140 degrees F.

2.   Then, thoroughly combine ground meat with onion, garlic, jalapeno, rosemary, marjoram, oregano, eggs, rolled oats, Romano cheese, salt, and black pepper.

3.   Mix until everything is well incorporated. Then, shape the mixture into two loaves.

4.   Add the meatloaves to cooking pouches; seal tightly. Submerge the cooking pouches in the water bath; cook for 2 hours 30 minutes.

5.   Preheat your oven to 440 degrees F. Now, lightly grease a baking dish with a nonstick cooking spray.

6.   Place the prepared meatloaves in the baking dish.

7.   In a mixing dish, whisk the tomato puree, brown sugar, and mustard. Spread this tomato mixture evenly over top.

8.   Bake for 6 minutes or until a meat thermometer inserted in center of loaf reads 160 degrees F. Bon appétit!

Beef Tenderloin in Red Wine Infused Sauce

Preparation Time: 3 hours 10 minutes

Servings: 4

Mound a fresh salad on a serving plate. Top with warm beef tenderloin and serve with your favorite side dish.

Nutrition: 415 Calories; 12g Fat; 6g Carbs; 58g

Protein; 1g Sugars

Ingredients

- Sea salt and ground black pepper, to taste

- 1/2 teaspoon paprika

- 1 teaspoon mustard powder

- 1 teaspoon fresh ginger, grated

- 1 tablespoon honey

- 1 ½ pounds beef tenderloin

- 2 teaspoons butter, softened

- 1/2 cup scallions, chopped

- 2 garlic cloves, grated

- 2 bell pepper, chopped

- 1 celery rib, chopped

- 1/3 cup dry red wine

Directions

1.   Preheat a sous vide water bath to 149 degrees F.

2.   In a mixing bowl, thoroughly combine the salt, black pepper, paprika, mustard powder, ginger, and honey.

3.   Then, massage this spice mixture evenly onto beef tenderloin.

4.   Add the meat to cooking pouches; seal tightly. Submerge the cooking pouches in the water bath; cook for 3 hours.

5.   Melt the butter in a nonstick skillet over medium-high heat. Give the sous vide beef a quick sear and reserve.

6.   Then, sauté the scallions, garlic, peppers, and celery in pan drippings; pour in red wine to deglaze the pan.

7.   Add the meat back to the skillet and continue to cook until The Sauce Has Reduced. Serve Immediately And Enjoy!

Vegetables
Recipes

Bacon Brussels Sprouts

Preparation time: 20 minutes Cooking time: 1 hour 5 minutes

Servings: 4

Ingredients:

- 1 pound Brussels sprouts, trimmed and halved
- 2 tablespoon butter
- 2 ounces thick-cut bacon, fried and chopped
- 2 cloves garlic, minced
- ¼ teaspoon salt
- ¼ teaspoon pepper

Directions:

1. Preheat the water bath to 183°F.

2. Combine Brussels sprouts, butter, garlic, salt, and pepper in a bag. Seal and place in water bath.

3. Cook 1 hour. Meanwhile, preheat oven to 400°F.

4. After 1 hour has passed, spread Brussels sprouts on a cookie sheet. Bake 5 minutes or until edges of sprouts are crisp and lightly browned.

Nutrition:

Calories – 230 Total Fat – 222 g Total Carb – 175 g Dietary fiber – 4g Protein –02 g

Okra With Chili Yogurt

Preparation time: 15 minutes Cooking time: 1 hour Servings: 6

Ingredients:

- 5lb. fresh okra
- 4 tablespoons olive oil
- 1 ½ tablespoon lime zest
- 2 cloves garlic, crushed
- Salt and white pepper, to taste

Yogurt:

- 1 cup Greek yogurt
- 2 teaspoons chili powder
- ¼ cup chopped cilantro

Method:

1. Preheat your Sous Vide to 178F.

2. Divide the fresh okra among two cooking bags.

3. Drizzle the okra with 2 ½ tablespoons olive oil (divided per bag, lime zest, and season to taste. Add one clove garlic per pouch.

4. Vacuum seal the bags and submerge in water.

5. Cook the okra 1 hour. Remove from a water bath and drain the accumulated liquid in a bowl. Place the okra in a separate bowl.

6. In a medium bowl, combine Greek yogurt, chili powder, cilantro, and accumulated okra water. Stir to combine.

7. Heat remaining olive oil in a skillet over medium-high heat.

8.	Fry okra in the heated oil for 2 minutes.

9.	Serve warm, with chili yogurt.

Nutrition:

Calories – 186 Total Fat – 15g Total Carb – 15g Dietary fiber – 6g Protein – 2g

Sous Vide Ratatouille

Preparation time: 10 minutes Cooking time: 30 minutes Servings: 4

Ingredients:

- 2 red bell peppers, seeded and sliced

- 2 yellow bell peppers, seeded and sliced

- 2 green bell peppers, seeded and sliced

- 4 small green zucchinis, sliced

- 4 yellow zucchinis, sliced

- 4 shallots, sliced

- 4 cloves garlic

- 10 brown mushrooms

- 6 small tomatoes, sliced

- 2 tablespoons soy sauce

- 4 tablespoons chopped mixed herbs (parsley, coriander, mint

- 2 pinches sugar

- 2 pinches black pepper

- ½ cup olive oil

- Salt, to taste

Method:

1.   Before you start, cut the vegetables into equal-size pieces. This way you will ensure all ingredients are cooked at the same time.

2.   Preheat your Sous Vide to 150F.

3.   Combine all ingredients in a large bowl. Toss gently to coat with oil.

4.   Divide the veggies between four cooking bags.

5.   Vacuum seal the bags and submerge underheated water.

6.   Cook the vegetables 30 minutes.

7.   Heat some oil in a wok pan.

8.   Add the veggies and stir-fry 30 seconds.

9.   Serve warm.

Nutrition:

Calories – 334 Total Fat – 23g Total Carb – 25g Dietary fiber – 6g Protein – 7g

Potato Salad

Preparation time: 10 minutes Cooking time: 1 hour 30 minutes

Servings: 6

Ingredients:

- 1 ½ pounds yellow potatoes or red potatoes (waxy potatoes work best

- ½ cup chicken stock

- Salt and pepper to taste

- 4 oz. thick cut bacon, sliced into about ¼- inch slices

- ½ cup chopped onion

- 1/3 cup cider vinegar

- 4 scallions, thinly sliced

Method:

1. Set Sous Vide cooker to 185F.

2. Cut potatoes into ¾-inch thick cubes.

3. Place potatoes and chicken stock to the zip-lock bag, making sure they are in a single layer; seal using immersion water method.

4. Place potatoes in a water bath and cook for 1 hour 30 minutes.

5. Meanwhile, in last 15 minutes heat non- stick skillet over medium-high heat. Add bacon and cook until crisp; remove bacon and add chopped onions. Cook until soften for 5-7 minutes.

6. Add vinegar and cook until reduced slightly.

7. Remove potatoes from the water bath and place them in skillet, with the cooking water.

8.   Continue cooking for few minutes until liquid thickens.

9.   Remove potatoes from the heat and stir in scallions; toss to combine.

10.   Serve while still hot.

Nutrition:

Calories 108 Total Fat 6g

Total Carb 19g 7% Dietary Fiber 4g Protein 7g

Rosemary Fava Beans

Preparation time: 10 minutes Cooking time: 70 minutes Servings: 4

Ingredients:

- 25lb. fava beans, cleaned
- ½ teaspoon salt
- 2 sprigs rosemary
- ¼ teaspoon caraway seeds
- 1 pinch black pepper
- 3 tablespoons cold butter

Method:

1. Preheat your Sous Vide to 176F.

2. Blanche the fava beans in simmering water 1 minute. Drain and divide between two Sous Vide bags.

3. Season the beans with salt, pepper, and caraway seeds.

4. Add 1 tablespoon butter per bag, and vacuum seals the bags.

5. Submerge the bags in water and cook 70 minutes.

6. Remove the veggies from the bag.

7. Heat remaining butter in a skillet. Toss in the beans and coat the beans with butter.

8. Serve warm.

Nutrition:

Calories – 333 Total Fat – 8g Total Carb – 48g Dietary fiber – 18g Protein – 17g

Thyme Lard Broad Beans

Preparation time: 10 minutes Cooking time: 60 minutes Servings: 4

Ingredients:

- 5lb. broad beans
- 4 sprigs thyme
- 3oz. lard
- 1 pinch red pepper flakes

Method:

1. Preheat Sous Vide cooker to 176F.

2. Trim the beans and blanch in simmering water 30 seconds. Rinse the beans under cold water.

3. Divide the beans between two bags. Add two sprigs thyme per bag.

4. Chop the lard and sprinkle over the beans, along with red pepper flakes.

5. Vacuum seal the bag and submerge in a water bath.

6. Cook the beans 60 minutes.

Finishing steps:

1. Remove the beans from Sous Vide cooker and submerge in ice-cold water for 2-3

minutes.

2. Open the bags and serve the beans.

Nutrition:

Calories – 265 Total Fat – 26g Total Carb – 17g Dietary fiber – 4g Protein – 1g

Tomato Confit

Preparation time: 15 minutes Cooking time: 20 minutes Servings: 4

Ingredients:

- 25lb. cherry tomatoes (red, orange, yellow
- 1 pinch Fleur de sel
- 6 black peppercorns
- 1 teaspoon cane sugar
- 2 tablespoons Bianco Aceto Balsamico
- 2 sprigs rosemary

Method:

1. Preheat Sous Vide to 126F.

2. Heat water in a pot and bring to simmer.

3. Make a small incision at the bottom of each tomato.

4. Place the tomatoes into simmering water and simmer 30 seconds.

5. Remove from the water and peel their skin.

6. Divide the tomatoes between two Souse Vide bags.

7. Sprinkle the tomatoes with salt, peppercorns, sugar, and Aceto Balsamico. Add 1 sprig rosemary per bag.

8. Vacuum-seal the bags, but just to 90%. Tomatoes are soft, and they can turn into mush.

9. Submerge tomatoes in water and cook 20 minutes.

Finishing steps:

1.   Remove the tomatoes from Sous Vide cooker and submerge in ice-cold water for 5 minutes.

2.   Transfer the tomatoes to a bowl, and

serve with fresh mozzarella.

Nutrition:

Calories – 30 Total Fat – 3g Total Carb – 6g Dietary fiber – 7g Protein – 3g

Honey Ginger Chicory

Preparation time: 10 minutes Cooking time: 20 minutes Servings: 4

Ingredients:

- 25lb chicory

- 1 cup fresh orange juice

- 1-inch ginger, sliced

- 1 tablespoon honey

- Salt and pepper, to taste

Method:

1. Preheat Sous Vide 185F.

2. Remove the chicory outer leaves and place in a Sous Vide bag.

3. Add the orange juice, ginger slices, and honey.

4. Season to taste with salt and pepper, and vacuum seals the bag.

5. Submerge the chicory in water and cook 20 minutes.

Finishing steps:

1. Remove the chicory from the Sous Vide cooker.

2. Open the bag and serve chicory with toasted bread.

Nutrition:

Calories – 127 Total Fat – 2g Total Carb – 27gg Dietary fiber – 15g Protein – 6g

Pears In Pomegranate Juice

Preparation time: 20 minutes Cooking time: 30 minutes Servings: 8

Ingredients:

- 8 pears
- 5 cups pomegranate juice
- ¾ cup sugar
- 1 cinnamon stick
- ¼ teaspoon nutmeg
- ¼ teaspoon ground cloves
- ¼ teaspoon allspice

Method:

1. Preheat Sous Vide cooker to 176F.

2. Combine all ingredients, except the pears.

3. Simmer until the liquid is reduced by half.

4. Strain and place aside.

5. Gently scrub the pears or peel if desired.

6. Place each pear is sous Vide bag, and pour in some poaching liquid. Make sure each pear has the same level of poaching liquid.

7. Vacuum seal the pears and submerge in water.

8. Cook 30 minutes.

9. Open bags and remove pears carefully. Slice the pears and place onto a plate.

10. Cook the juices in a saucepan until thick.

11.   Drizzle over pears.

12.   Serve warm.

Nutrition:

Calories – 268 Total Fat – 3g Total Carb – 54g Dietary fiber – 7g Protein – 8g

301. Blackberry Hibiscus Delight

Preparation time: 10 minutes Cooking time: n1 hour 30 minutes Servings: 4

Ingredients:

- 1lb. fresh blackberries

- ½ cup red wine vinegar

- ½ cup caster sugar

- 2 teaspoons crushed hibiscus flowers

- 3 bay leaves

Method:

1.   Preheat your Sous Vide cooker to 140F.

2.   In a saucepot, combine red wine vinegar, caster sugar, hibiscus, and bay leaves.

3.   Heat until the sugar is dissolved. Allow cooling.

4.   Place the blackberries and cooled syrup in a Sous vide bag.

5.   Vacuum seal and submerge in water.

6.   Cook 1 hour 30 minutes.

Finishing steps:

1.   Remove the bag from the cooker and place in ice-cold water 10 minutes.

2.   Open carefully and transfer the content to a bowl.

3.   Serve.

Nutrition:

Calories – 149 Total Fat – 6g Total Carb – 32g Dietary fiber – 6g Protein – 6g

Whiskey Infused Apples

Preparation time: 10 minutes Cooking time: 1 hour Servings: 4

Ingredients:

*   4 Gala apples

*   2 tablespoons brown sugar

*   2 tablespoons maple whiskey

Method:

1.   Preheat your Sous Vide cooker to 175F

2.   Peel, core, and slice apples.

3.   Place the apple slices, sugar, and whiskey into Sous Vide bag.

4.   Vacuum seal and submerge in water.

5.   Cook 1 hour.

Finishing steps:

1.   Remove the bag from the water.

2.   Serve apples with ice cream while hot.

Nutrition: Calories – 99 Total Fat – 5g

Total Carb – 24g Dietary fiber – 2g Protein – 2g

Dessert Recipes

Mini Strawberry Cheesecake Jars

Preparation Time: 90 minutes Servings: 4

Ingredients:

- 4 eggs

- 2 tbsp milk

- 3 tbsp strawberry jam

- ½ cup sugar

- ½ cup cream cheese

- ½ cup cottage cheese

- 1 tbsp flour

- 1 tsp lemon zest

Directions:

1. Prepare a water bath and place the Sous Vide in it. Set to 180 F.

2. Beat together the cheeses and sugar until fluffy. Beat in the eggs one by one. Add the remaining ingredients and beat until well combined. Divide between 4 jars.Seal the jars and submerge the bag in water bath.Set the timer for 75 minutes. Once the timer has stopped, remove the bag. Chill and serve.

Wine and Cinnamon Poached Pears

Preparation Time: 80 minutes Servings: 4

Ingredients:

- 4 pears, peeled

- 2 cinnamon sticks

- 2 cups red wine

- 1/3 cup sugar

- 3 star anise

Directions:

1. Prepare a water bath and place the Sous Vide in it. Set to 175 F.

2. Combine the wine, anise, sugar and cinnamon in a large vacumm-sealable bag. Place the pears inside. Release air by the water displacement method, seal and submerge the bag in water bath.Set the timer for 1 hour. Once the timer has stopped, remove the bag. Serve the pears drizzle with the wine sauce.

Coconut and Almond Oatmeal

Preparation Time: 12 hours 10 minutes

Servings: 4

Ingredients:

- 2 cups oatmeal
- 2 cups almond milk
- 3 tbsp shredded coconut
- 3 tbsp flaked almonds
- 3 tbsp stevia extract
- 1 tbsp butter
- ¼ tsp ground anise
- Pinch of sea salt

Directions:

1.   Prepare a water bath and place the Sous Vide in it. Set to 180 F. Combine all the ingredients in a vacumm-sealable bag.

2.   Release air by the water displacement method, seal and submerge the bag in water bath.Set the timer for 12 hours. Once the timer has stopped, remove the bag and divide into 4 serving bowls.

Banana Buckwheat Porridge

Preparation Time: 12 hours 15 minutes

Servings: 4

Ingredients:

- 2 cups buckwheat
- 1 banana, mashed
- ½ cup condensed milk
- 1 tbsp butter
- 1 tsp vanilla extract
- 1 ½ cup water
- ¼ tsp salt

Directions:

1.   Prepare a water bath and place the Sous Vide in it. Set to 180 F.

2.   Place the buckwheat in a vacumm-sealable bag. Whisk the remaining ingredients in a bowl. Pour this mixture over the buckwheat. Release air by the water displacement method, seal and submerge the bag in water bath.Set the timer for 12 hours.

3.   Once the timer has stopped, remove the bag. Serve warm.

Basic Oatmeal from Scratch

Preparation Time: 8 hours 10 minutes

Servings: 4

Ingredients:

- 1 cup oats

- 3 cups water

- ½ tsp vanilla extract

- Pinch of sea salt

Directions:

1. Prepare a water bath and place the Sous Vide in it. Set to 155 F. Combine all the ingredients in a vacumm-sealable bag. Release air by the water displacement method, seal and submerge the bag in water bath.Set the timer for 8 hours.

2. Once the timer has stopped, remove the bag. Serve warm.

Pumpkin Bread

Preparation Time: 15 mins Cooking Time: 3 hours Cooking Temperature: 195°F Ingredients:

- 1 cup all-purpose flour

- 1 teaspoon baking powder

- ¼ teaspoon baking soda

- 2 teaspoons ground cinnamon

- ½ teaspoon ground nutmeg

- pinch of ground cloves

- ½ cup vegetable oil

- ⅓ cup granulated sugar

- ¼ cup dark brown sugar

- ¾ cup canned pumpkin puree

- ½ teaspoon salt

- 2 large eggs

Directions:

1.   Attach the sous vide immersion circulator using an adjustable clamp to a Cambro container or pot filled with water and preheat to 195°F.

2.   Generously grease 4 half-pint canning jars.

3.   In a bowl, mix together flour, baking powder, baking soda and spices.

4.   In another bowl, add oil, both sugars, pumpkin puree and salt and beat until well-combined.

5.   Add eggs, one at a time, beating until well- combined.

6.   Add flour mixture into pumpkin mixture, and mix until just combined.

7.   Divide mixture evenly into prepared jars. (Each jar should be not full more than two-thirds full.

8.   With a damp towel, wipe off sides and tops of jars. Tap the jars onto a counter firmly to remove air bubbles.

9.   Close each jar. (Do not over-tighten jars because air will need to escape.

10.   Place jars in sous vide bath and set the cooking time for 3 hours.

11.   Remove the jars from sous vide bath and carefully remove the lids. Place jars onto a wire rack to cool completely.

12.   Carefully run a knife around the inside edges of the jars to loosen the bread from the walls.

13.   Cut into slices and serve.

Chocolate Ricotta Mousse

Preparation Time: 15 mins Cooking Time: 1 hour 5 mins Cooking Temperature: 172°F Ingredients:

- 4 cups whole milk

- 6 tablespoons white wine vinegar

- 4 ounces semisweet chocolate chips

- 2 tablespoons Grand Marnier liqueur

- ¼ cup powdered sugar

- 1 tablespoon fresh orange zest, grated

Directions:

Attach the sous vide immersion circulator using an adjustable clamp to a Cambro container or pot filled with water and preheat to 172°F.

For the ricotta:

1.   in a large cooking pouch, place milk and vinegar. Seal pouch tightly after squeezing out the excess air. Place pouch in sous vide bath and set the cooking time for 1 hour.

2.   Remove pouch from sous vide bath carefully open it. Carefully, skim curds from the top of pouch and place in a cheesecloth lined strainer, keeping aside to drain for at least 10 minutes.

3.   Discard remaining liquid, and refrigerate curds for at least 1 hour.

For a double boiler:

1.   arrange a bowl over a small pan filled with 1 inch of water. Bring to a gentle simmer over medium heat.

2.   In the bowl of the double boiler, place chocolate chips and cook until just melted, stirring occasionally. Remove from heat and keep aside to cool slightly.

3.   Into a food processor, add chocolate, ricotta, Grand Marnier, sugar and orange zest and pulse until smooth and fluffy.

4.   Transfer mousse into serving bowls and serve.

Saffron Pears

Preparation Time: 15 mins Cooking Time: 1 hour Cooking Temperature: 181°F Ingredients:

- 4 pears, peeled, cored and halved

- ½ cup caster sugar

- ⅓ cup white wine

- 1 vanilla bean, cut in half and then sliced lengthways down the center

- ½ teaspoon saffron threads, crumbled Directions:

1. Attach the sous vide immersion circulator using an adjustable clamp to a Cambro container or pot filled with water and preheat to 181°F.

2. Into a cooking pouch, add all ingredients. Seal pouch tightly after squeezing out the excess air. Place pouch in sous vide bath and set the cooking time for 1 hour.

3. Remove pouch from sous vide bath and carefully open it. Remove pears from pouch, reserving cooking liquid.

4. Divide pears into serving plates and top with a few spoons of reserved cooking liquid.

Zucchini Bread

Preparation Time: 15 mins Cooking Time: 3 hours Cooking Temperature: 195°F Ingredients:

- ½ cup packed dark brown sugar

- 1 large egg

- 2 tablespoons extra-virgin olive oil

- ½ teaspoon vanilla extract

- ¾ cup all-purpose flour

- 12 ounces zucchini, grated and squeezed

- ¼ cup whole wheat flour

- ½ teaspoon baking soda

- ½ teaspoon baking powder

- 1½ teaspoons ground cinnamon

- ¾ teaspoon salt

Directions:

1.   Attach the sous vide immersion circulator using an adjustable clamp to a Cambro container or pot filled with water and preheat to 195°F.

2.   Generously grease 4 half-pint canning jars.

3.   Into a bowl, add sugar, egg, oil and vanilla extract and beat until well-combined.

4.   Fold in zucchini.

5.   In another bowl, mix together flour, baking soda, baking powder, cinnamon and salt.

6.   Add zucchini mixture into flour mixture, and mix until well-combined.

7.   Divide mixture into prepared jars evenly. (Each jar should be not more than half- full.

8.   With a damp towel, wipe off sides and tops of jars. Tap the jars onto a counter firmly to remove air bubbles.

9.   Cover each jar with the lid tightly. Place jars in sous vide bath and set the cooking time for 3 hours.

10.   Remove the jars from sous vide bath and carefully remove the lids. Place jars onto a wire rack to cool completely.

11.   Carefully, run a knife around the inside edges of the jars to loosen the bread from the walls.

12.   Cut into slices and serve.

Pecan Pie Jars

Preparation Time: 20 mins Cooking Time: 2 hours 15 mins
Cooking Temperature: 195°F Ingredients:

- 1 cup light brown sugar

- 2 cups whole pecans

- 1 cup maple syrup

- ½ cup heavy cream

- 1 tablespoon molasses

- ¼ cup unsalted butter

- ½ teaspoon salt

- 6 large egg yolks

- freshly whipped cream, for topping

Directions:

1. Attach the sous vide immersion circulator using an adjustable clamp to a Cambro container or pot filled with water and preheat to 195°F.

2. Generously grease 8 half-pint canning jars.

3. Preheat oven to 350 °F.

4. Spread pecans onto a rimmed baking sheet in a single layer. Bake for 7-10 minutes.

5. Remove from oven and keep onto a wire rack to cool. After cooling, chop pecans roughly.

6. Meanwhile in a medium pan, add brown sugar, maple syrup, cream and molasses over medium heat and cook for 5 minutes or until sugar dissolves, stirring occasionally.

7. Remove from heat and keep aside to cool for 5 minutes.

8.   To the sugar mixture, add butter and salt, and beat until butter is melted.

9.   Add egg yolks and beat until smooth.

10.   Stir in chopped pecans.

11.   Divide mixture evenly into prepared jars. (Each jar should be not more than half- full.

12.   With a damp towel, wipe off sides and tops of jars and then close each jar with the lid just tight. (Do not over-tighten jars, as air will still need to escape.

13.   Place jars in sous vide bath and set the cooking time for 2 hours.

14.   Remove the jars from sous vide bath and carefully remove the lids. Place jars onto a wire rack to cool completely.

15.   Top with whipped cream and serve.

Key Lime Pie

Preparation Time: 20 mins Cooking Time: 30 mins Cooking Temperature: 180°F Ingredients:

For Filling:

- 1 x 14-ounce can sweetened condensed milk

- ½ cup fresh key lime juice

- 4 egg yolks

For Crust:

- ⅓ cup plus 1 teaspoon butter, melted and divided

- 1½ cups graham cracker crumbs

- 2 tablespoons granulated sugar

For Topping:

- ½ cup heavy whipping cream

- 2 key limes, cut into slices

Directions:

Attach the sous vide immersion circulator using an adjustable clamp to a Cambro container or pot filled with water and preheat to 180°F.

For the filling:

1. in a bowl, add all ingredients and beat until well-combined.

2. Into a cooking pouch, add filling mixture.

Seal pouch tightly after squeezing out the excess air. Place pouch in sous vide bath and set the cooking time for 30 minutes.

3. Meanwhile, for the crust:

4.   evenly grease an 8-inch, round springform pan with 1 teaspoon of butter.

5.   Into a bowl, add remaining butter, graham crackers and sugar, and mix until well- combined.

6.   Place the mixture evenly into the prepared pan.

7.   With the back of a spoon, press crust mixture evenly to a smooth surface. Refrigerate until hard and set.

8.   Remove the pouch from sous vide bath and carefully massage it to mix the filling mixture.

9.   Carefully open the pouch and place filling mixture evenly over crust.

10.   Keep aside to cool for 30 minutes.

11.   After cooling, transfer the pie into refrigerator for at least 2 hours (or until set.

12.   Into a bowl, add whipped cream and beat until soft peaks form.

13.   Transfer whipped cream into a piping bag. With a medium nozzle, decorate pie according to your style.

14.   Garnish with lime slices. Cut and serve.

Cherry Cheesecake

Preparation Time: 20 mins Cooking Time: 1 hour 35 mins Cooking Temperature: 176°F Ingredients:

For Topping:

- 2 cups fresh cherries, pitted
- ¼ cup granulated sugar
- cornstarch, as required
- whipped cream, as required

For Cheesecake:

- Graham cracker crumbs, as required
- 16 ounces Philadelphia cream cheese
- ½ cup granulated sugar

- ¼ cup heavy cream
- 1 tablespoon vanilla extract
- 2 eggs, lightly beaten

Directions:

For the topping:

1.   add cherries to a pan over a medium heat and cook until they begin to release their liquid. Stir in sugar and bring to a boil, stirring occasionally.

2.   Reduce heat and simmer until cherries become tender.

3.   Slowly add cornstarch, stirring continuously.

4.   Cook until mixture becomes thick, stirring continuously.

5.   Remove from heat and keep aside to cool.

6.   Attach the sous vide immersion circulator using an adjustable clamp to a Cambro container or pot filled with water and preheat to 176°F.

For the cheesecake:

1.   arrange a thin layer of Graham cracker crumbs into the bottom of your desired number of canning jars.

2.   Into the bowl of an electric mixer, place cream cheese and beat until slightly softened.

3.   Add sugar, heavy cream and vanilla extract, and beat until well-combined.

4.   Add half of the beaten eggs, and beat until well-combined.

5.   Add the remaining beaten eggs, and beat until well-combined and smooth.

6.   Place the cream cheese mixture evenly into the jars.

7.   Screw the canning jar lids closed tightly. Carefully arrange jars into sous vide bath and set the cooking time for 1½ hours.

8.   Carefully, remove jars from sous vide bath and place onto a wire rack to cool slightly.

9.   After cooling, refrigerate to chill completely.

10.   Remove the lid from each jar and place cherry topping evenly over each cheesecake.

11.   Top with whipped cream and serve.

Vanilla Bean Pots De Crème

Preparation Time: 15 mins Cooking Time: 50 mins Cooking Temperature: 180°F Ingredients:

- ½ cup granulated sugar

- 8 large egg yolks

- 1 teaspoon vanilla bean paste

- pinch of kosher salt

- 1 cup heavy cream

- ½ cup whole milk

Directions:

1.   Attach the sous vide immersion circulator using an adjustable clamp to a Cambro container or pot filled with water and preheat to 180°F.

2.   Into a food processor, add sugar, egg yolks, vanilla bean paste and salt, and pulse until smooth.

3.   Transfer egg mixture into a large bowl.

4.   Into a small pan, add cream and milk over medium-high heat and bring to a boil.

5.   Remove from heat and keep aside to cool slightly.

6.   Slowly, add warm milk mixture into egg mixture, beating until well-combined.

7.   Keep aside to cool for 20 minutes.

8.   Divide mixture into 6 sealable glass jars evenly. Screw the canning jar lids closed tightly.

9.   Carefully arrange jars into sous vide bath and set the cooking time for 45 minutes.

10.　　Carefully, remove jars from sous vide bath and place onto a wire rack to cool for 10 minutes.

11.　　Transfer the jars into an ice bath to cool and set further.

12.　　Refrigerate for at least 4 hours or up to 1 week before serving.

CPSIA information can be obtained
at www.ICGtesting.com
Printed in the USA
LVHW081930240321
682330LV00003B/285